The Body Tour

Here are some of the most amazing facts and figures about the body you're walking around in.

by Cameron Fusillio

ETA® Cuisenaire

800-445-5985
www.etacuisenaire.com

The Body Tour
ISBN 0-7406-4159-X
ETA 383201

ETA/Cuisenaire • Vernon Hills, IL 60061-1862
800-445-5985 • www.etacuisenaire.com

Series © 2006 by ETA/Cuisenaire®

Original version published by Nelson Australia Pty Limited (2002).
This edition is published by arrangement with Thomson Learning
Australia.

ETA/Cuisenaire
Manager of Product Development: Mary Watanabe
Creative Services Manager: Barry Daniel Petersen
Production Manager: Jeanette Pletsch
Lead Editor: Betty Hey
Copy Editor: Barbara Wrobel
Production Artist: Diana Chiropolos
Graphic Designer: Amy Endlich

Photographs on pp. 5, 7–8, 14, 17–18, 25, 27, and cover by
Fotograffiti
Illustrations on pp. iv, 1–3, 5–6, 9–12, 15–16, 19–24, 27, and cover
by Guy Holt Design

Teacher consultant: Garry Chapman, Ivanhoe Grammar School

Printed in China.

06 07 08 09 10 11 12 13 14 15   10 9 8 7 6 5 4 3 2 1

Contents

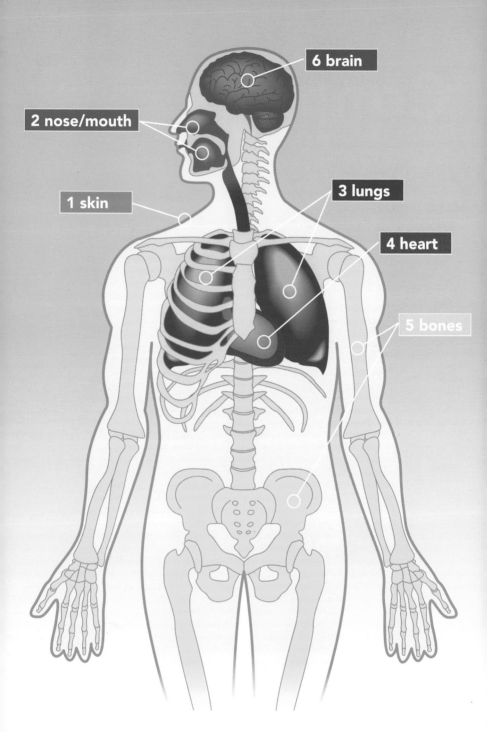

6 brain

2 nose/mouth

1 skin

3 lungs

4 heart

5 bones

Chapter One

It's All in the Skin

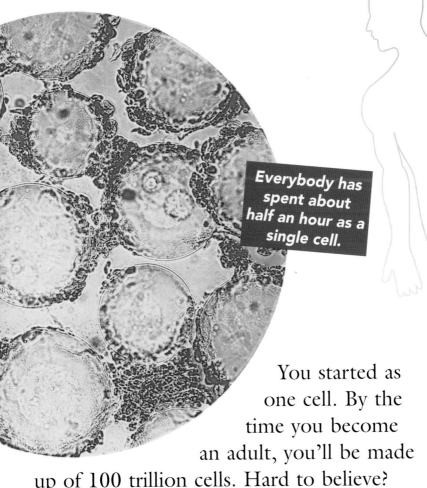

Everybody has spent about half an hour as a single cell.

You started as one cell. By the time you become an adult, you'll be made up of 100 trillion cells. Hard to believe? Let's take a **tour** of your body in action.

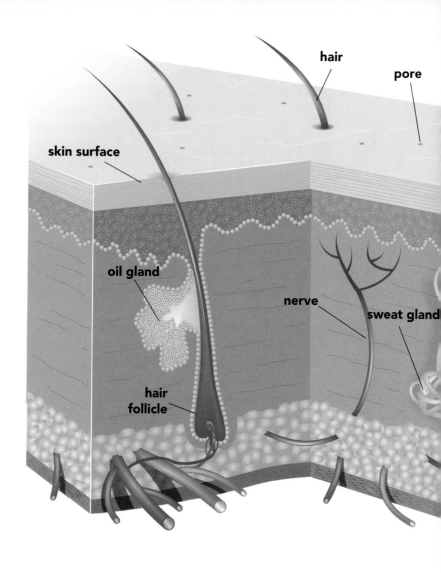

hair

pore

skin surface

oil gland

nerve

sweat gland

hair follicle

Starting from the outside and working in, the first stop is your skin. The skin is the biggest **organ** in your body.

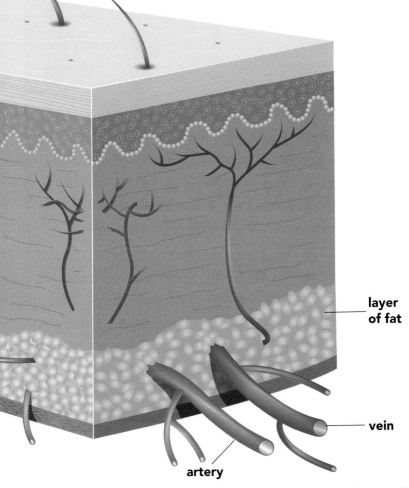

layer
of fat

vein

artery

As well as giving you your sense of touch, the skin protects you against germs, knocks, heat, and cold. Without it, your body would fall apart.

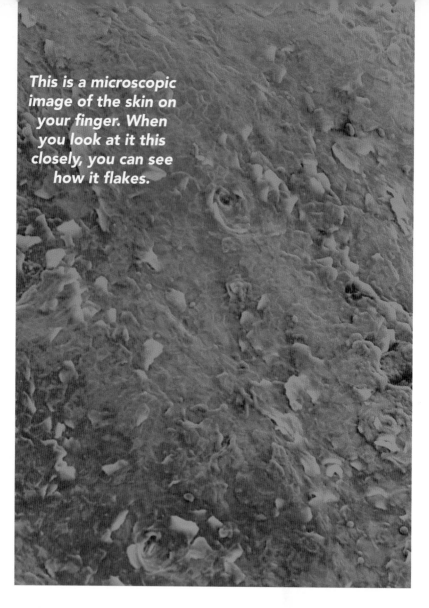

This is a microscopic image of the skin on your finger. When you look at it this closely, you can see how it flakes.

Every 15 to 30 days, your body replaces the whole outside layer of your skin. It doesn't come off all at once. It just flakes away little by little.

Chapter Two

The Nose Knows

For the next stop
on our tour, we're
going inside.

One way inside is
through your nose.
Yuck!

5

The average human will breathe about 20,000 times in the next 24 hours.

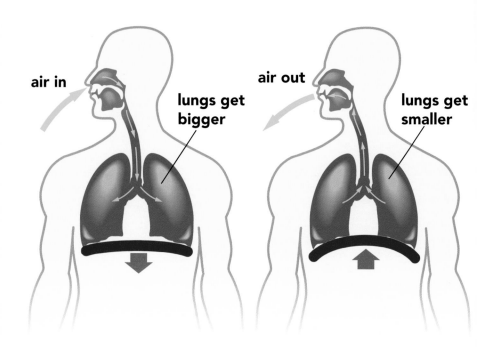

air in

lungs get bigger

air out

lungs get smaller

Your nose has two nostrils. They let you breathe in air that goes to your lungs. It's a bit sticky inside your nostrils.

Sticky **mucus** lines the inside of your nose. It protects your lungs from the dirt that is in the air you breathe.

Your nose makes nearly a cupful of snot every day.

Many people call mucus snot. Snot works by trapping the dust and germs in the air you breathe and keeping them in the nose—till you sneeze them out.

The speed of your sneeze can be up to 100 miles per hour. Now that's fast!

Ahhhhhh-choooo! When you sneeze, everything stops for a moment—even your heart. And you can't keep your eyes open either. Try it!

Your nose can detect up to 10,000 different smells, but your tongue can detect only four different kinds of flavors.

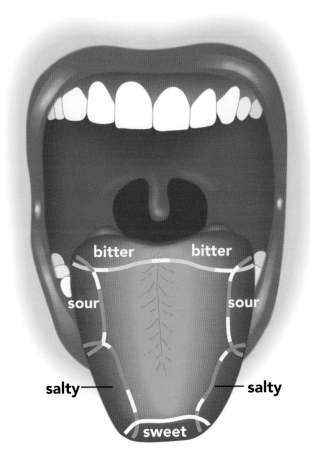

If we don't get sneezed out, our tour continues downwards through the mouth. When your nose smells food, it makes your mouth water.

Let's stop for a closer look at the mouth.

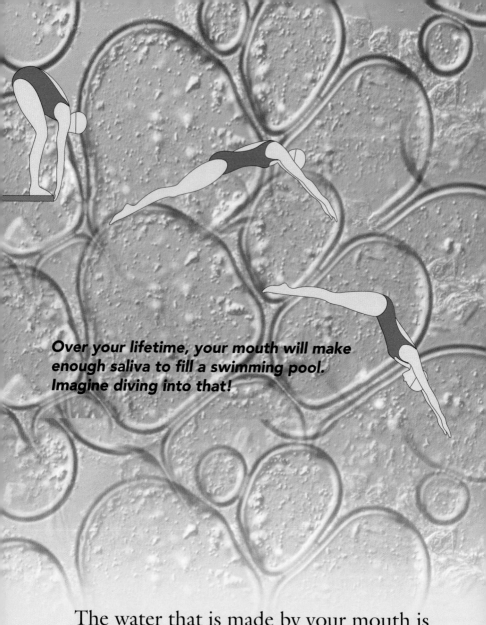

Over your lifetime, your mouth will make enough saliva to fill a swimming pool. Imagine diving into that!

The water that is made by your mouth is called saliva. Saliva helps break down food as you chew it. Like snot, it protects your mouth from germs.

Chapter Three

Sucked In

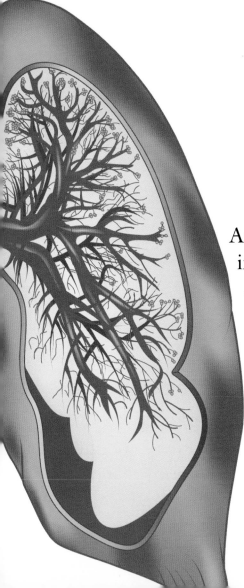

Another breath in and we're being sucked down into the lungs. Lungs are important because they absorb **oxygen**. We need oxygen to stay alive. Cells also need oxygen to make energy.

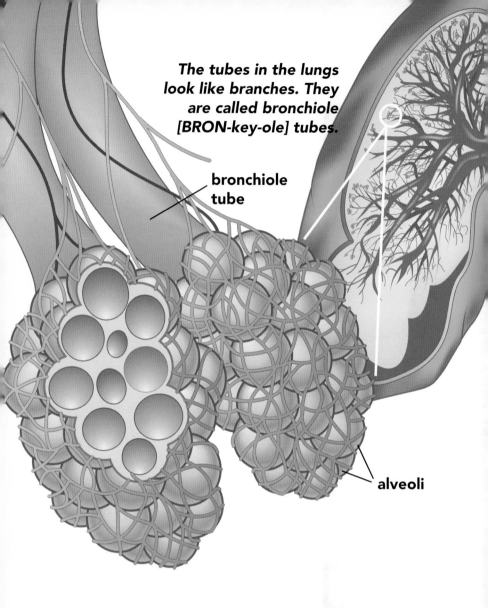

The tubes in the lungs look like branches. They are called bronchiole [BRON-key-ole] tubes.

bronchiole tube

alveoli

The lungs are a network of tubes. As we go deeper and deeper into the lungs, the tubes keep dividing and getting narrower and narrower. Come down with us and see.

The alveoli make your lungs look like a giant pink sponge.

There are 600 million alveoli in the lungs.

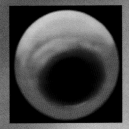

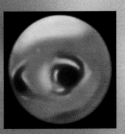

Finally, we're inside a tiny sac. These sacs are called alveoli [al-VEE-oh-lie]. The alveoli are the places where the oxygen that we breathe enters the blood.

A cough almost sends us speeding out of the lungs at close to 60 miles an hour.
But what's that huge beating noise nearby?

Chapter Four

Have a Heart

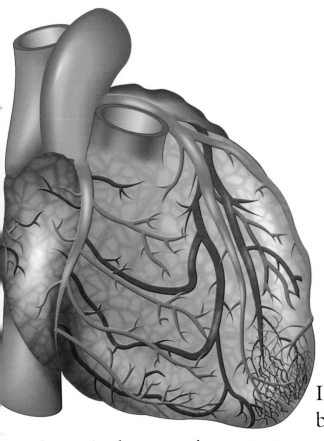

It's the heart beating. Your heart is the most important **muscle** in your body. Its job is to pump blood full of oxygen to every part of your body.

How does it work?

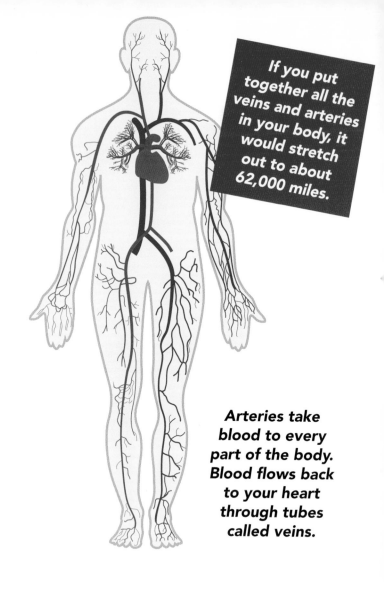

Arteries take blood to every part of the body. Blood flows back to your heart through tubes called veins.

Blood full of oxygen from the lungs flows to the heart. Then the heart pushes the blood through a huge network of tubes called arteries [ART-er-ees].

Your heart is about the same size as a clenched fist. Hold your fist up to your chest and see.

Unlike the other muscles in your body, your heart never has a rest. It pumps all day and night.

The average human heart beats about 70 times in a minute and more than 100,000 times a day.

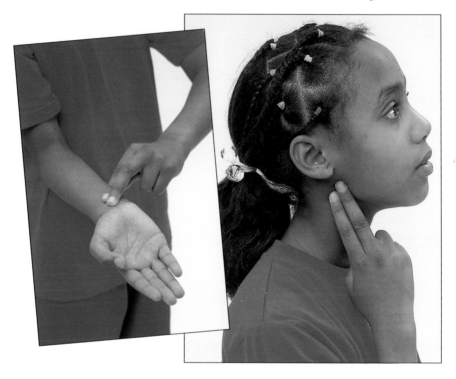

You can feel a jet of blood when you count your heartbeats. The best places to feel it beating are on your wrist and your neck.

This is where the blood is pumping through your arteries. The beating of the heart is called a pulse.

Next stop, your ribcage.

Chapter Five

Count the Bones

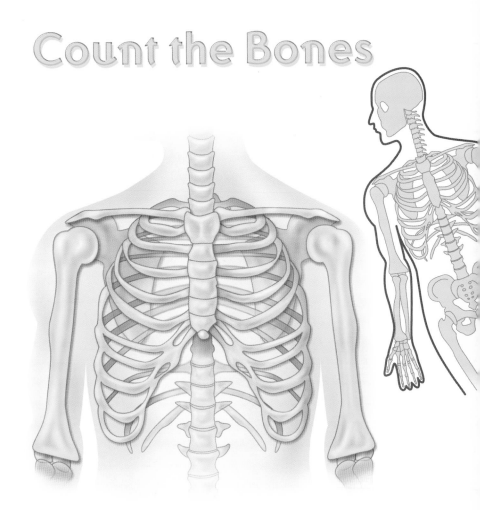

Your rib bones protect the organs in your chest. You have 24 ribs, with 12 ribs on each side. See if you can feel them all.

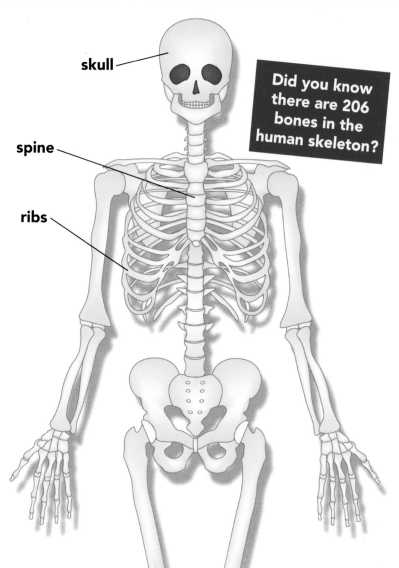

skull

spine

ribs

Did you know there are 206 bones in the human skeleton?

Your bones hold you up. Without them your body would just be floppy skin, muscles, and organs.

While we're in here, let's check out the rest of your **skeleton**.

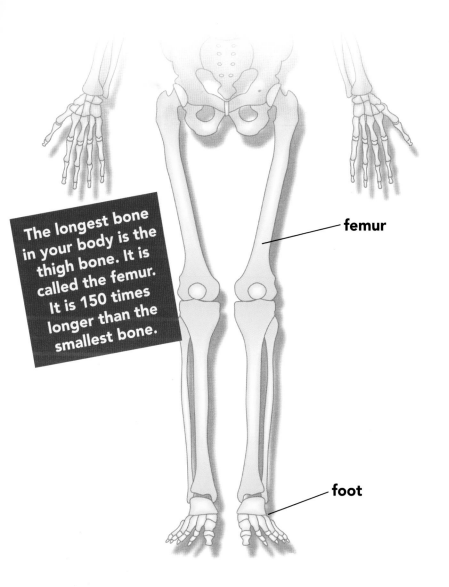

The longest bone in your body is the thigh bone. It is called the femur. It is 150 times longer than the smallest bone.

femur

foot

We'll begin the skeleton tour at your feet. Count the bones. There are 26 bones in each foot. There are also 26 bones in your spine from bottom to top.

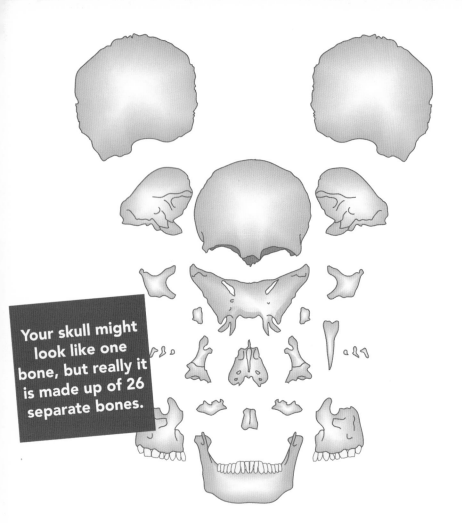

Your skull might look like one bone, but really it is made up of 26 separate bones.

Inside your **skull**, you will find the smallest bone in your body. It isn't one of your head bones. It is inside your middle ear.

As you can see, bones come in lots of different shapes and sizes.

It's not far to go to our next stop—inside your skull.

Chapter Six

Head Full

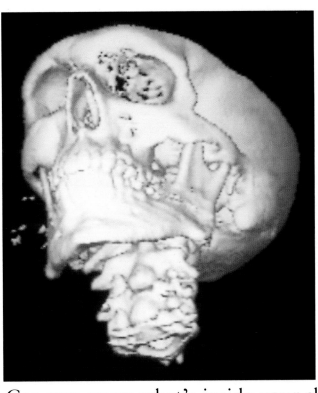

Can you guess what's inside your skull?
It's your brain, of course. Your brain is so
important, it is protected by the solid case
of the skull.

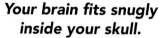

Your brain fits snugly inside your skull.

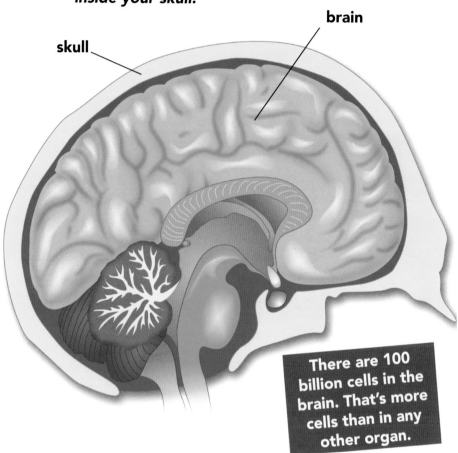

brain

skull

There are 100 billion cells in the brain. That's more cells than in any other organ.

Your brain is like your body's computer. It is where you do all your thinking. It is also the part that lets you feel and it is in charge of your senses. It gets information from all over your body.

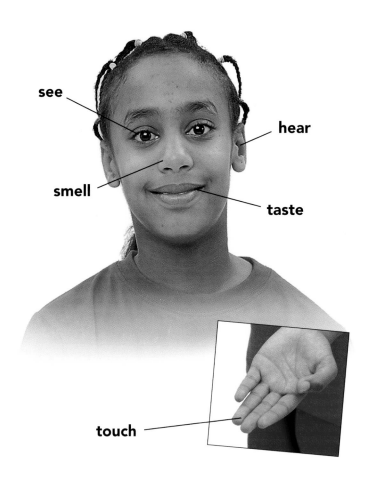

see

hear

smell

taste

touch

Your brain is helped out by your five senses. Your brain sends messages to your body when you taste, smell, touch, hear, and see. It is the brain that puts this information together and tells you how to behave.

The eyeball is attached to the skull by six long muscles. This means the eye can look in different directions and send messages to the brain at the same time.

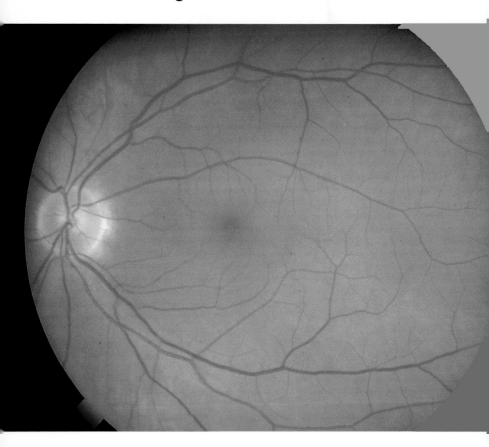

Whoops! We're sliding down to the eyeball. You can see everything from here. Your eyes are the windows of the brain. Your eyes receive light signals and tell you what you see.

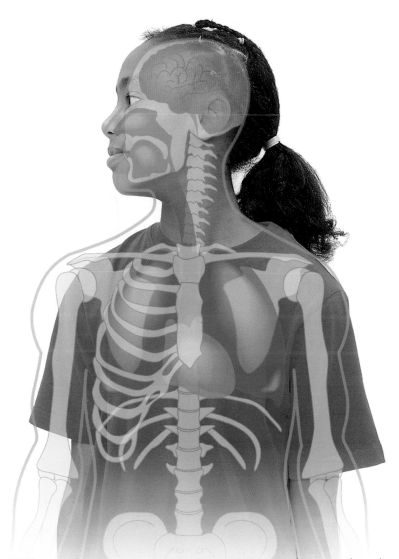

Wow, that was amazing! We're almost back to where we came in.

That ends our tour of your body in action. As you can see, there was a lot to discover. We hope you enjoyed the ride.

Glossary

mucus thick, slimy liquid produced in the body

muscle a part of the body which gives you strength and power to move

organ a part of the body, such as the skin, heart, or stomach, that has a particular job to do

oxygen a gas which is part of the air we breathe

skeleton all the bones in a body

skull the bones of the head

tour to travel from one place to another

Index